CARVING THE HEAD
in the Classic European Tradition

CARVING THE HEAD
in the Classic European Tradition

Martin Geisler-Moroder

Geisler-Moroder
Austrian Woodcarving School

Fox
Chapel Publishing
1970 Broad Street • East Petersburg, PA 17520
www.FoxChapelPublishing.com

Alan Giagnocavo
Publisher

Peg Couch
Acquisition Editor

Gretchen Bacon
Editor

Troy Thorne
Design and Layout

Horst Pali
Step-by-Step Artwork

Zita Baracsi
Text and Photography

Carving the Head in the Classic European Tradition is an original work, first published in 2006 by Fox Chapel Publishing Company, Inc. The patterns contained herein are copyrighted by the author. Readers may make three copies of these patterns for personal use. The patterns themselves, however, are not to be duplicated for resale or distribution under any circumstances. Any such copying is a violation of copyright law.

ISBN-13: 978–1–56523–302–7
ISBN-10: 1–56523–302–6

Publisher's Cataloging-in-Publication Data

Geisler-Moroder, Martin.

    Carving the head in the classic European tradition / Martin Geisler-Moroder. -- East Petersburg, PA : Fox Chapel Publishing, c2006.

        p. ; cm.

        ISBN-13: 978-1-56523-302-7
        ISBN-10: 1-56523-302-6
        A reference guide from the instructors at the Geisler-Moroder Austrian Woodcarving School.

    1. Wood-carving--Technique. 2. Wood-carving--Patterns.
    3. Head in art. 4. Busts. 5. Wood sculpture--Technique. I. Title.

TT199.7 .G45 2006
736/.4--dc22   0605

To learn more about the other great books from
Fox Chapel Publishing, or to find a retailer near you,
call toll-free 1-800-457-9112 or visit us at **www.FoxChapelPublishing.com**.

Note to Authors: We are always looking for talented
authors to write new books in our area of woodworking, design,
and related crafts. Please send a brief letter describing your idea to
Peg Couch, Acquisition Editor, 1970 Broad Street, East Petersburg, PA 17520.

Printed in China
10 9 8 7 6 5 4 3 2 1

Acknowledgments

As this book was the result of teamwork at the Geisler-Moroder Austrian Woodcarving School, I wish to thank the following instructors: Michael Bachnetzer, Pascal Wirth, Gottfried Kaschning, Robert Simon, Markus Treml, Claudia Grutsch, Bernhard Tragut, Werner Schneider, and Walter File.

A very special thanks is extended to Horst Pali, an instructor at the Geisler-Moroder Austrian Woodcarving School, who carved the project on which this book is based.

Table of Contents

About the Author and the Artist --- **viii**

Preface --- **x**

Part One: Getting Started --- **1**

An introduction to the process --- 1

Tools and materials -- 3

Wood --- 4

Safety -- 4

Theory --- 4

Part Two: Step-by-Step Modeling -- **9**

Making the armature --- 10

Geometrical building blocks --- 11

Geometrical shaping -- 13

The first modeling cuts --- 17

The finished model -- 20

Part Three: The First Stage of Carving --- **25**

Before the first cut --- 26

Cutting the profile view -- 28

Fixing the profile --- 29

Cutting the first planes --- 32

The planes of the neck --- 34

Part Four: The Second Stage of Carving --- **37**

Setting the forms of the nose, the mouth, and the chin ------------------------------------ 38

Setting the forms of the eyes and the hairline -- 40

The sides of the head, the shoulders, and the collar --------------------------------------- 44

Carving the back -- 45

Part Five: The Third Stage of Carving --- **49**

Detailing the nose, the mouth, and the chin --- 50

Shaping the ears -- 53

The finishing touches: the hair, the collar, and the base ---------------------------------- 56

Part Six: The Final Finish – A Gallery of Ideas -- **59**

Appendix A – Metric Conversion Chart -- **72**

Appendix B – Illustrations --- **73**

About the Author and the Artist

Martin Geisler-Moroder
and family

**Geisler-Moroder Austrian
Woodcarving School**
A-6652 Elbigenalp 63
Lechtal, Austria
Tel. +43 5634 6215
Fax: +43 5634 6128
geisler-moroder@aon.at
www.woodcarvingschool.com

The Geisler-Moroder Austrian Woodcarving School

The tradition of woodcarving has been passed on from generation to generation in the Moroder family for over 400 years. At the beginning of the 1950s, Professor Rudolf Geisler-Moroder began to teach woodcarving to a group of young students in Elbigenalp, Austria. This was the seed of the school that today is called the Geisler-Moroder Austrian Woodcarving School.

The professor's son, Martin Geisler-Moroder, established the present school in 1984. It is not only the largest school of its kind, where creative people from five continents come to learn the art of woodcarving, but also the only school that follows a "dual-system education" in the field of carving. Practical and theoretical lessons are taught in parallel during the weekly courses. All courses are bilingual, presented in both German and English, and are available at all levels. The participants can find suitable courses in any area of woodcarving, including figure and ornamental carving. This list of classes includes portraits, nude figures, animals, relief, decorations, rough outs, nativity figures, and many more. Specialized courses, such as modeling, chainsaw carving, stone and bronze sculpturing, woodturning, painting, and gilding—to mention only a few—are also among the possible choices.

Many of those who carve as a hobby spend their holidays in Elbigenalp, participating in short courses and benefiting from both the high-quality courses and the beauty of the surrounding Alps. For those who wish to pursue woodcarving as a career, the school offers a longer-term structured curriculum to prepare for the Professional Wood-Sculptor Diploma. Classes are held all year round.

There are special "English weeks" organized for those who wish to meet other English-speaking carvers. These classes combine woodcarving courses with sightseeing tours and other social activities.

Martin Geisler-Moroder and his family welcome all course participants to enjoy their comfortable guesthouse and their excellent restaurant. For information on courses, please contact the Geisler-Moroder Team at the address at the left.

About the Instructor Who Completed the Project

Horst Pali was born in 1965 in St. Johann/Tyrol, Austria. He studied woodcarving for four years in the government Woodcarving School in Elbigenalp and graduated as a Wood Sculptor in 1985. He is a self-employed sculptor and a carving instructor at the Geisler-Moroder Austrian Woodcarving School. He specializes in the restoration of churches.

Horst lives with his wife, Maria, and his two sons in their family home in Tyrol.

Horst Pali, an instructor at the school, carved the project for this book.

Preface

The history of woodcarving goes back to the early ages, and woodcarving has continued to grow and thrive as a handicraft today. Much of its success can be attributed to the continued development of the tools and techniques of the trade, allowing for contemporary interpretations of diverse themes in woodcarving. Believing in the constant need for growth, the Geisler-Moroder Austrian Woodcarving School has created contemporary carving methods that help to push woodcarving to the next level.

However, even the specialized knowledge in the Geisler-Moroder Austrian Woodcarving School is based on a rich and longstanding tradition. The Geisler-Moroder family has spent over 400 years in the field of woodcarving arts and crafts. Here, preserved tradition and new teaching and learning methodology have merged.

A hallmark of the Geisler-Moroder Austrian Woodcarving School's method is working with planes and surfaces, which is described step-by-step in this book. Based on the theories of proportion, it is possible to approach the realistic representation of the human head. This method also teaches a special way of observation; at all times during the process of carving, the carver learns to see the object of the carving as if it were composed of cubical forms. Additionally, in this book, a wide range of possibilities for the refinement of details is given.

A solid artistic technique is the foundation for every high-quality piece of art. That is why the goal of this book is to present easy-to-understand visual instructions for mastering the carving of the human head. The step-by-step instructions provide the groundwork for the basic composition of your piece, and the examples in the gallery at the back of the book offer you ideas and inspiration. Once you have completed the step-by-step project and have learned the techniques, you will be able to extend the skills acquired to your other projects.

We wish you much success in creating your artwork and encourage you to let your own ideas flow!

Part One
Getting Started

Getting a good picture of the finished carving in your mind before you start carving (and keeping it there throughout the process) is an important step in creating the final project. With that in mind, we will begin our discussion with the detailed modeling and go over the entire carving process.

An introduction to the process

Working from the picture, we will first build an armature to make a firm foundation for the clay model. The actual modeling will start with rolling simple geometrical shapes, which we will form through various steps to create a satisfactory three-dimensional model of the head to use as an example for our carving.

The Geisler-Moroder Austrian Woodcarving School Way

We work with planes, and this technique is the main difference that distinguishes our school from other schools of carving. We always search to visualize and carve the inclusive geometrical forms.

Carvers are often inclined to skip this important preparation by using ready-made models and other figures to copy in wood. We would like to put an emphasis on originality because we believe that, through creating original pieces of work, woodcarving becomes a more meaningful experience for the carver and a more respected and valued activity in the world of art and craft. However, if you already have a suitable model prepared, you may start directly with the carving process on page 25, leaving out the modeling part of the project.

Modeling, similar to sketching, may at first cause difficulties for some craftsmen and craftswomen who claim to be able to carve anything in wood if they have a model to follow. Modeling is an additive technique of sculpturing (the form is created by adding material), while carving is a subtractive technique (the form is created by cutting away material). To make the process of modeling easier for carvers, we will use a mixture of additive and subtractive techniques that will imitate carving in some parts, making the process more familiar for carvers. So have courage and follow us!

After modeling, we will guide you through three stages of carving, clearly indicating where each stage will lead. The first stage will begin with roughing out the main shape, except the back of the head. In the second stage, we will cut more detailed planes and carve the back of the head. In the third stage, the planes will clearly shape some finer features of the face.

After completing the third stage of carving, you may already hold in your hands a beautiful carving. The planes will lend a modern feel to it. You may decide to finish the process at this stage. However, some carvers may like to continue on to experiment with different styles. In the gallery section of our book, found on page 59, we will show variations on the same sculpture, including a selection of finishing techniques in realistic and stylized forms. There are many useful tips for carvers in this part. However, we cannot emphasize enough the importance of individual creativity and the value of a bold, exploring mind.

Let's start!

The Geisler-Moroder Austrian Woodcarving School Way

Leaving the back untouched allows flexibility for carvers to correct mistakes and—in case of an emergency—even cut the face a second time if necessary.

Tools and materials

At right is a list of the tools and materials used in modeling and carving the project demonstrated in this book. Our instructor, Horst, used 80 mm wide #1 chisel and #8 gouge from the Stubai collection. He prefers working with wide Stubai tools; however, this is a personal choice. If you don't have these special tools, 30 to 50 mm #1 chisel and #8 gouge are equally suitable. Even though we recommend the Stubai collection, as a general rule, use the tools you have! (If you would like to purchase Stubai tools, contact the Geisler-Moroder Austrian Woodcarving School or your nearest carving supply store for purchasing information.)

The band saw is one of the few power tools that we use because of its timesaving benefits. If you do not have access to a band saw, consider commissioning your local carpenter to prepare the wood for you.

Tools and Materials

Chisels and gouges
- #1-30 mm chisel
- #1-40 mm chisel
- #2-20 mm chisel
- #3-16 mm gouge
- #3-40 mm gouge
- #5-16 mm gouge
- #5-30 mm gouge
- #7-10 mm gouge
- #7-20 mm gouge
- #8-20 mm gouge
- #8-40 mm gouge
- #9-10 mm gouge
- #11-10 mm gouge
- #11-30 mm gouge

Additional tools
- Calipers
- Mallet
- Carving screw
- Modeling knives
- Wire-end modeling tool
- Pencil
- Band saw

Materials
- Modeling clay, approximately 9 lbs.
- Wood for armature base, 1³⁄₁₆" x 7¹⁄₁₆" x 8¹¹⁄₁₆"
- Wood of choice for armature supporting pole, 1³⁄₁₆" x 1³⁄₁₆" x 8¹¹⁄₁₆"
- 2 ½"-diameter dowels, 5½" long and 3⅛" long
- Block of wood suitable for carving, 5¹⁵⁄₁₆" x 6⁵⁄₁₆" x 10¼"

3

Wood

We used a block of cembra pine for carving. It has a light, appealing color, and it is soft. Its grain structure is regular, and, if well seasoned, it has no tendency to split. Cembra pine is very pleasant to carve, and, because it is native to Tyrol, our carvers often choose to sculpt it. Sugar pine or basswood is an equally fine choice for this project. Use good-quality wood; lesser-quality wood is harder to carve, and the frustration you experience will not be worth the small amount of money you saved.

Safety

Woodcarving can be dangerous, and safety should be in your mind at all times.

Make it a rule to keep your tools sharp. Sharp tools cut the wood with less force and consequently do less damage if they slip. Your cuts in the wood will also be more exact, and you will spend less time cleaning up unwanted gouge marks at the end.

Take frequent breaks. A well-balanced carving process not only reduces the risk of accident, but also allows the carver to have the necessary "distance" from the piece in order to see it from new perspectives. Be sure to cover the cutting edges of the tools when they are not in use.

Theory

A firm foundation in theory is important for all carvers. When trying to achieve a good-quality carving of a human head, a basic understanding of the proportion and anatomy of the human head can make a significant difference. A "right feeling" for balance and proportion is part of our aesthetic senses. Sometimes artists use unharmonious proportions to create a special effect. However, such a choice should be based on a deep understanding of theoretical principles.

In Europe, the Geisler-Moroder Austrian Woodcarving School is the unique provider of the "dual-system education" in the field of woodcarving. Our students receive an additional program alongside their practical training. In these additional lessons, we not only provide the necessary basics in proportion, anatomy, mimic, modeling, designing skills, and art history, but also make it possible for our students to widen their practical skills by taking lessons from other areas of sculpting and traditional crafts. These additional lessons are all organized around a well-structured theory curriculum.

You will notice, as you are working through this book, that much of the theory relevant to carving the human head is outlined within the project. Here, we would like to offer an additional brief overview.

The Geisler-Moroder Austrian Woodcarving School Way

We highly recommend that carvers familiarize themselves with correct techniques of tool sharpening before starting the project. At the Geisler-Moroder Austrian Woodcarving School, sharpening is such an important skill that each instructor addresses it in all of his classes.

Anatomy and Proportion of the Human Head

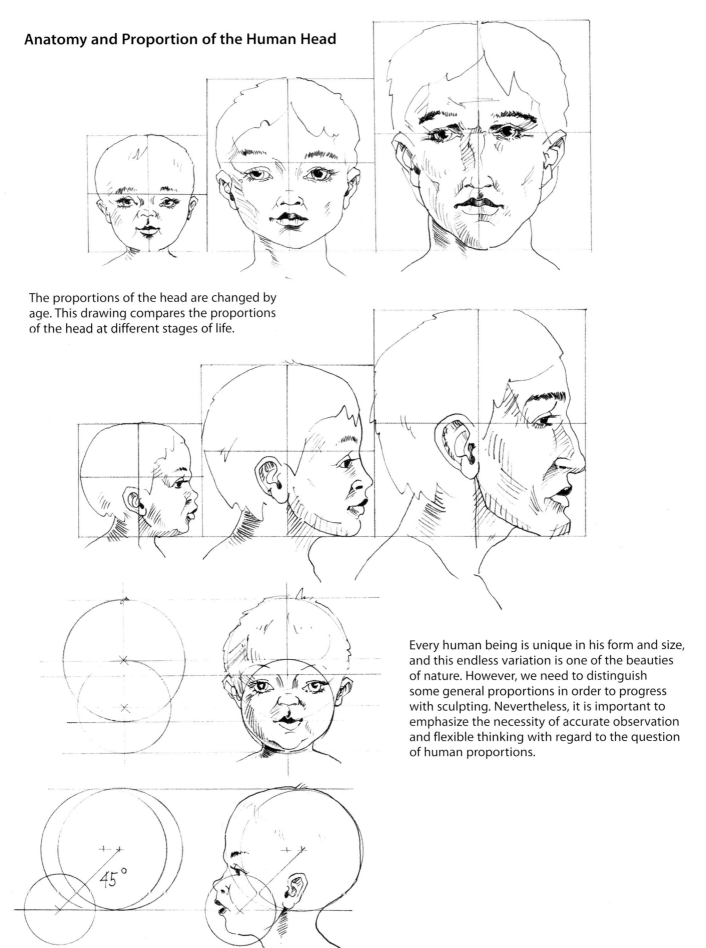

The proportions of the head are changed by age. This drawing compares the proportions of the head at different stages of life.

Every human being is unique in his form and size, and this endless variation is one of the beauties of nature. However, we need to distinguish some general proportions in order to progress with sculpting. Nevertheless, it is important to emphasize the necessity of accurate observation and flexible thinking with regard to the question of human proportions.

The Aging Face

2 years

18 years

40 years

95 years

As people get older, the basic features of the face change dramatically. Wrinkles appear around the eyes, the flesh becomes less springy, and the mouth becomes less full and embedded in wrinkles. Deep furrows run from the nose to the corners of the mouth, and the nose grows longer. The hook-nosed witch of fairy tales is an exaggeration of this biological process.

The changes to facial features that are brought about by age have to be considered when carving the human head. The above illustration should help you to visualize the process, which can be divided into four basic stages, more clearly.

Facial Expressions

When our emotions change, our facial expressions change as well.

At a comprehensive level, the emotional expressions of the human face are mapped with the help of simple sketches, making the emotional changes of the face more understandable. Here we would like to introduce some of these basic maps to assist you in the further study of the head.

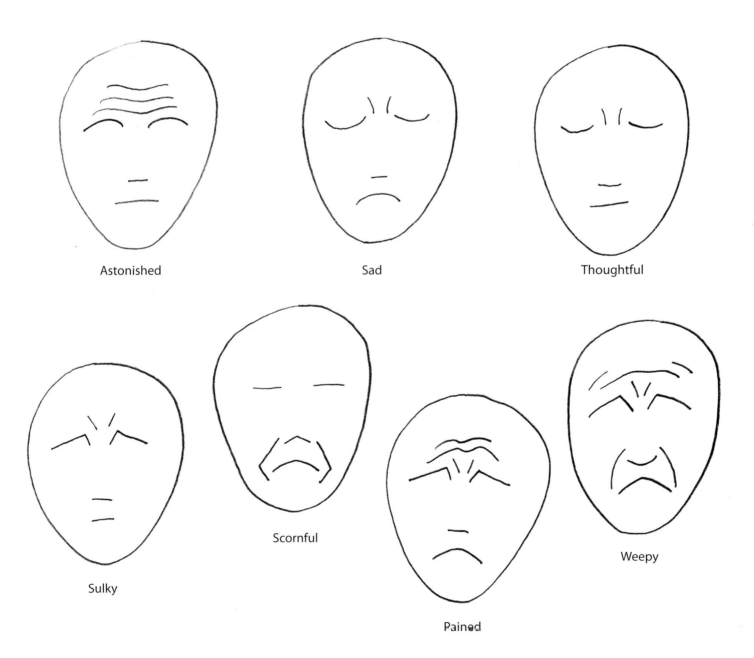

Astonished

Sad

Thoughtful

Sulky

Scornful

Pained

Weepy

Part Two
Step-by-Step Modeling

The following steps will take you from the initial sketch to the finished clay model. Although you may be inclined to skip this section, avoid the temptation. Modeling your project before you begin the actual carving is a great way to work through any difficult parts and to infuse the project with your own style.

Tools and Materials
- Modeling clay, approximately 4 kg (9 lbs.)
- Wood of choice for base, 1 3/16" x 7 1/16" x 8 11/16"
- 2 1/2"-diameter dowels, 5 1/2" long and 3 1/8" long
- Wood of choice for supporting pole, 1 3/16" x 1 3/16" x 7 11/16"
- Calipers
- Modeling knives
- Wire-end modeling tool
- Pencil

Part Two: Step-by-Step Modeling

Making the armature

The first step of modeling is to make an accurate armature. The armature not only holds the modeling clay firmly, but also sets the foundation for the correct proportions of the figure.

▶**1** Cut the pieces of wood according to the measurements given in the diagram. Make a 45-degree cut on one end of the supporting pole.

▼**2** Drilling holes and using gouges to widen the hole, cut a 1³⁄₁₆" x 1³⁄₁₆" square hole on the base. The hole should be about ¹³⁄₁₆" to 1³⁄₁₆" deep, or enough to make the pole stable. Glue the supporting pole in the hole. (Or, cut the pole shorter and attach the pole to the base with a screw from the bottom. There is no need to make a hole for this alternative method.)

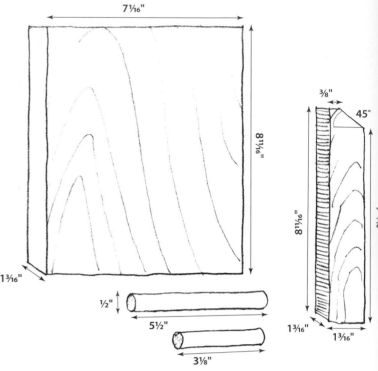

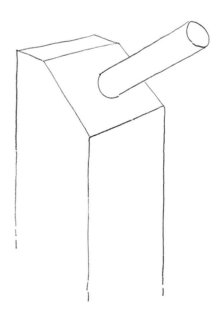

▲**3** Drill two ½" holes on the pole for the dowels: one at the top for the shorter dowel, the other 2³⁄₈" up from the bottom for the longer dowel. The shorter dowel is for the head; this hole should be drilled ¹³⁄₁₆" deep at a 45-degree angle to the supporting pole. The longer dowel will support the shoulders; this hole should be drilled at a 90-degree angle to the pole completely through the pole.

◄ **4** The finished armature is very simple, but it will be just what we need to support the weight of the clay model.

Geometrical building blocks

The actual modeling begins with creating geometrical building blocks from modeling clay, such as Plasticine, that correspond to different sections of the figure. We will build these geometrical building blocks on the armature.

▶**5** First make a 5½" x 3⅛" x 2¾" rectangular block for the shoulders from modeling clay.

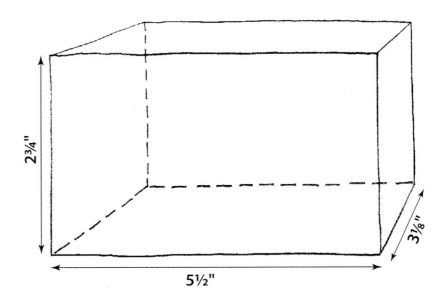

◀ **6** Check the position of the dowel in the shoulder block. The dowel should not protrude from the block at all. Also, make sure that the shoulder block is the correct height.

▼ **7** Make a cylinder for the neck from modeling clay, according to the given measurements.

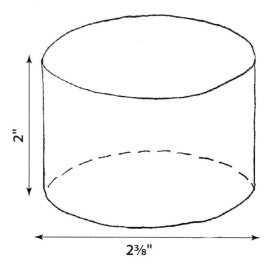

▼ **8** After positioning the neck and the shoulder blocks, use a modeling knife to mark the vertical centerline on the bust. (We will call it a "guideline" in order to differentiate it from the centerline that will halve the face.) This guideline will indicate the vertical center of the whole figure, while the centerline will mark only the center of the face. If the figure is facing front, these two lines are the same. If the head of the figure turns (as in our case), the two lines do not match. Understanding the relationship between these two lines is important in order to correctly transfer the position of the model to the wood.

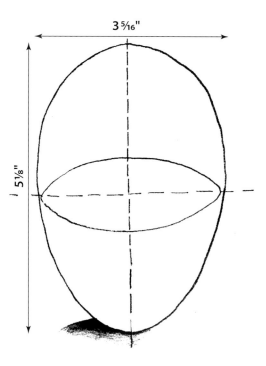

▲ **9** Traditionally, we think of the human head as an upside-down egg shape. The widest spot on the skull is at the upper third. Form an egg for the head from modeling clay based on the measurements given in the diagram. Ensure that the egg is perfectly symmetrical to the vertical axis or distortion will appear in the model at a later stage. Incise the vertical centerline with a knife.

▲**10** Turn the egg upside down and push the dowel through the side of the egg that is closest to the thinner end.

▲**11** The centerline of the head is about 30 degrees to the right of the extended guideline. The head should appear to be turning to the right. The neck is simply a cylinder tilted slightly forward. The geometrical building section is complete.

Geometrical shaping

In this section, we will use geometrical shapes to approximate the facial features of the model. We will form basic shapes for the nose, the mouth, the chin area, the jaws, and the ears.

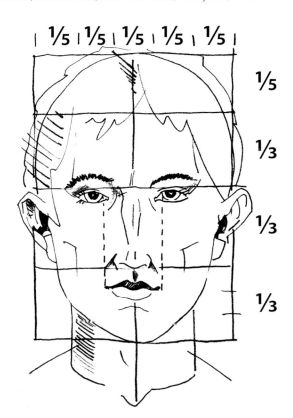

▲**12** Across the centerline of the head, incise a horizontal line with a knife at about one-fifth of the height down from the top of the head to set the hairline. Divide the remaining length into three equal parts, and mark every part with a horizontal line. The upper line will determine the position of the eyes; the lower line will mark the tip of the nose and the opening of the mouth. (Please see the detailed theory on the proportion of the human head on pages 80 and 81.)

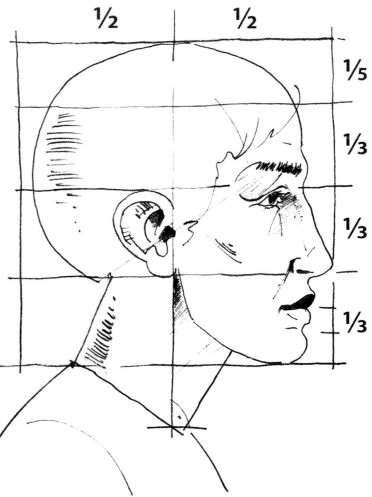

▲ **13** Add some more modeling clay to the mouth and chin/jaw area and shape it.

▼ **14** Refer to the illustrations in Step 12 and at the right to place the ear. The vertical line and the second and third horizontal lines show how the ear is aligned with the nose. Affix the ears and the jaws to the model.

Creating Geometrical Shapes

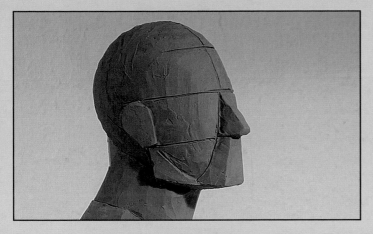

Some carvers find that they have difficulty creating the geometrical shapes for the facial features of the model. The following tips may help. Use these tips just to get started. As you gain more experience, you, too, will be able to place features by "feel."

For the ears: Form a shallow rectangular block. Cut a symmetrical heart shape that touches the edges of the rectangle. Split the heart shape in half. Cut off ⁹⁄₁₆" from the tip of the heart. The two big parts of the heart will be the ears.

For the jaws: Cut two triangles from the larger pieces of the leftover rectangle. These triangles are approximately equal-sided with one of the angles about 120 degrees.

For the nose, mouth, and chin: Shape a long pyramid. Cut 15 mm off the top of the pyramid. Starting at the base of the remaining piece, cut halfway up the pyramid. Make a horizontal cut where the vertical cut ends. Discard the smaller shape. Fit the bigger shape on the head to form the nose, mouth, and chin area.

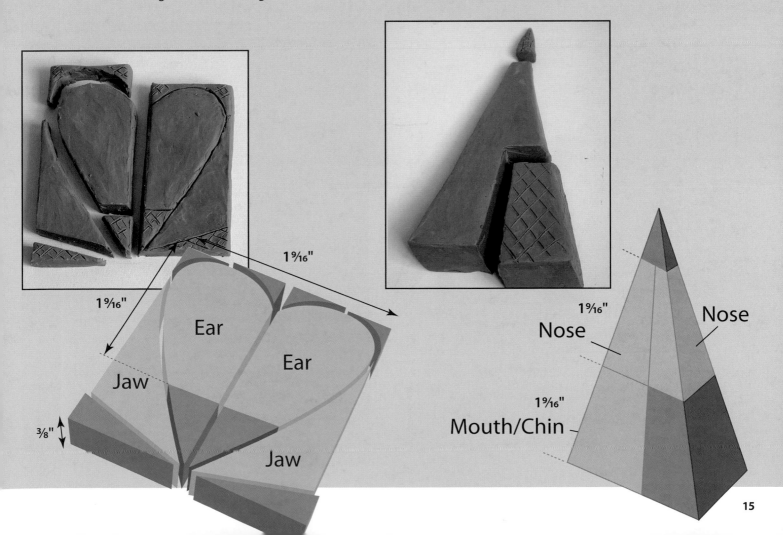

◄ 15 After positioning the basic shapes, build up the shoulders by affixing two wedges of modeling clay on the rectangular block. The wedges tuck up against the neck cylinder.

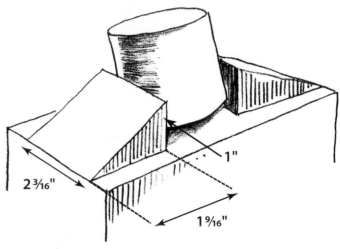

▶ 16 To complete the foundations of modeling, we need to mark additional proportion lines in the mouth/chin area. Divide the lowest third of the head (along the centerline) into three parts, and incise two lines with a knife: one for the mouth, the other for the hollow of the chin.

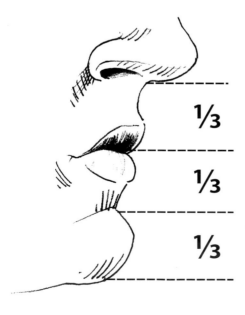

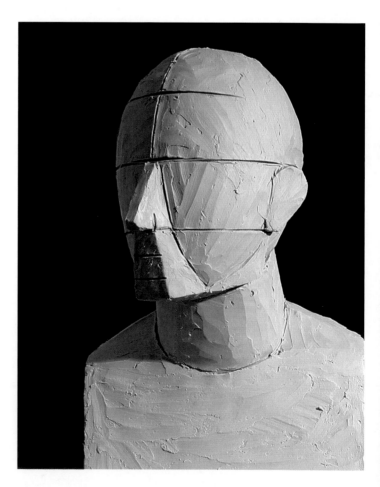

▼ ▶ **17** The geometrical shaping is complete. It is now time to prepare the model for the first modeling cuts.

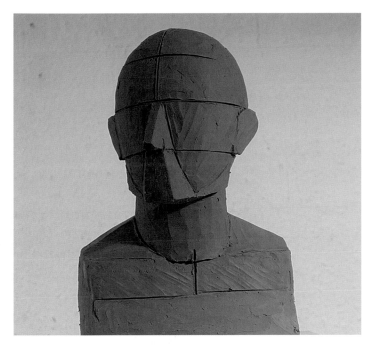

The first modeling cuts

Now that the basic shapes have been added to the geometrical building blocks, the model needs to be prepared for the first modeling cuts. For this stage of modeling, a mirror may prove useful to double-check the model's features against your own.

▶ **18** Start by rounding the shoulders. Once the shoulders are rounded, deepen the hollow of the chin, making a "gouge" cut along the line closest to the base of the chin. Then, turn your attention to the eyes.

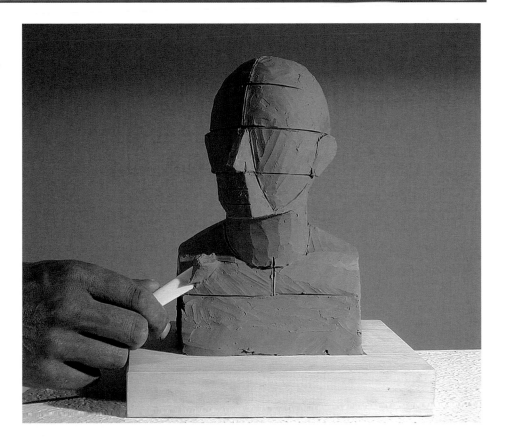

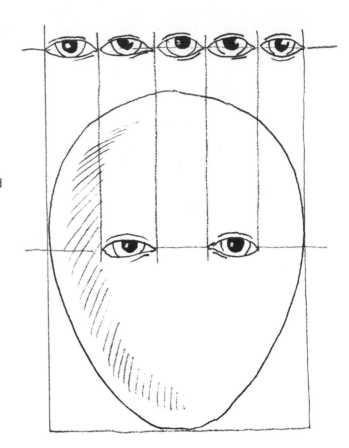

▶ **19** The eyes should be positioned under the second proportional line. If you divide the width of the head into five vertical parts (each part is the width of an eye), the eyes should be placed in the second and the fourth sections.

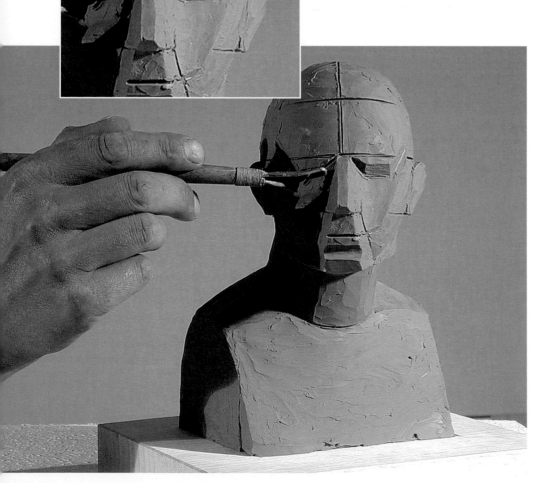

◀ **20** Using a wire-end tool, shape each eye as three planes, and then lower the cheeks under the eye. The basic shape of the eyes should appear to bulge out of the head (see inset).

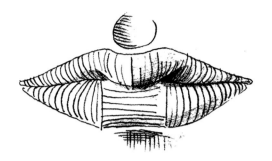

▶**21** When cutting the mouth, the volume of the lips should be emphasized. Also, the sweep of the mouth is not flat; rather, it is a crescent shape that runs between the two edges of the basic shape of the mouth/ chin. There is a slight depression at the corners of the mouth.

◀**22** Emphasize the hairline by removing some modeling clay from the forehead and the temples. Raise the muscles that run from the ears along the neck by removing the excess material from the front of the neck. This is also the right time to model a V-shaped neck for the shirt.

The finished model

23 To give the final shape to the nose, narrow the width of the bridge and slightly lower the area under the nose. Shape the channel with a gentle gouge cut. As you can see in the diagram, at least half of the nose sits on the face. It is often a typical mistake to place the nose too far out of the face. **Note:** Under the nose, the shape is round, not straight.

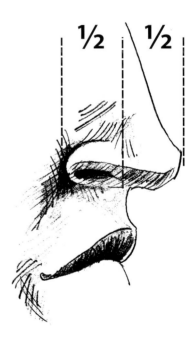

24 Deeper round cuts should indicate the wings of the nose. Those lines that connect the wings of the nose and the corners of the mouth (smile lines) run along the edges of the original shape. **Note:** Emphasize, just slightly, the smile lines between the wings of the nose and the corners of the mouth by lowering the area under the nose.

▶ **25** Shape the eyes so that they become rounded. Notice that they do not sit flat in the face; their surface is round like a peach stone, and the opening is narrow like an almond. In a profile view, it is clearly visible how far the corner of the eye should come around the face. Also note that the eyeball is tilted slightly forward and that the lower eyelid is behind the upper eyelid. These are areas of common mistakes for beginners.

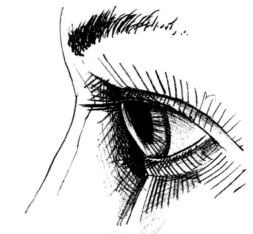

▼ **26** The ears slope inward from the widest point at the back of the ear down to the cheek at the front. Level the area of the ears near the cheeks, and round the outside edges. To indicate the inner ear, draw a hook-shaped line that sits on a small half circle, and deepen the inside of the ear along this line. It might also help to visualize the ears as two circles, as it is sketched below.

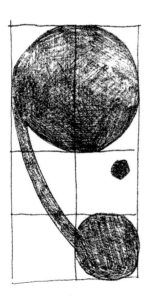
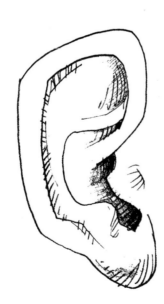

▶ **27** Last, with a few dynamic, sweeping lines, indicate the texture of the hair.

▶ **28** To finalize the model, smooth the face gently and clean up the rough cuts with the round end of the modeling knife. You don't need to give it the perfect finish that is needed for a model that was prepared for casting. Keep in mind that time is also an important factor in this endeavor. This model is designed to help you in the carving process; give it only as much attention as serves its purpose.

Optional Details

On these pages, we have included some optional details that may prove helpful for those who wish to pursue an ultra-realistic style. Two areas of the model can be detailed for an ultra-realistic look: the collar and the hair.

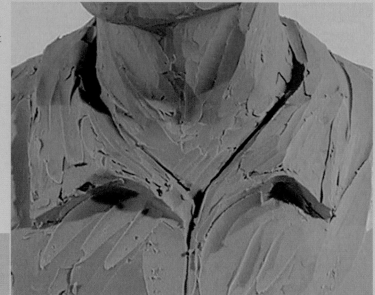

▲ **The collar:** To indicate the collar, add modeling clay at the front of the bust. Form the collar at an angle; then, turn the model around and follow the line of the collar. Add more modeling clay on the back above the collar's line and shape it accordingly.

◀ **The hair:** Change the sweep of the hairline slightly to lead the hair farther into the forehead. Cut the thick tresses of the hair to set the basic shapes first, and only then add the finer lines.

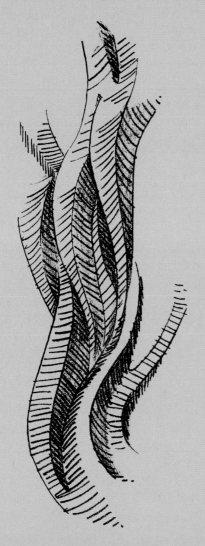

◀ **To texture the hair**, cut wavy lines with the modeling knife. To achieve a natural effect, make sure that the waves do not run parallel to each other; instead, the next wave should have already started before a wave smoothes away. From time to time, the soft waves should start or end in a sharp V-cut. The overall effect of the hair should not be regular but playful and dynamic.

▶ The finished model with optional details.

Part Three
The First Stage of Carving

The following steps will take you from the initial wood block to a bust with the initial planes carved. In this section, we will be roughing out the carving, leaving the back untouched. Not carving the back allows the carver the flexibility to correct any mistakes if needed. As we rough out the head, we will be using the geometric plane method that distinguishes our system from others. Working in planes will allow you to see the proportions of the face clearly as you go.

Tools and Materials
- #3-40 mm gouge
- #11-30 mm gouge
- Other chisels and gouges of choice
- Calipers
- Mallet
- Carving screw
- Pencil
- Band saw
- Block of wood suitable for carving,
  5¹⁵⁄₁₆" x 6⁵⁄₁₆" x 10¼"

Part Three: The First Stage of Carving

Before the first cut

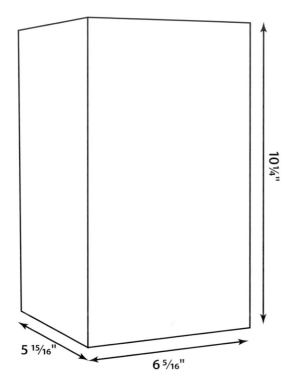

10¼"

5 ¹⁵⁄₁₆"

6 ⁵⁄₁₆"

◀ **1** After you have purchased the block of wood, cut the block according to the measurements shown in the diagram. Plane the wood so it is square on all sides. It is especially important that the bottom of the block forms perfect right angles with the sides.

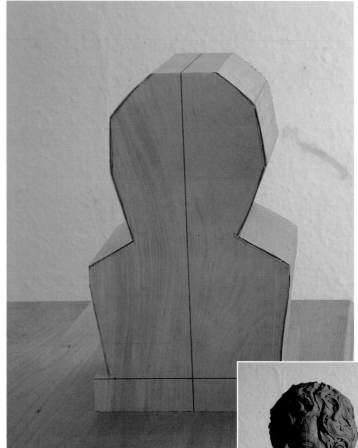

▼**2** Draw the band saw pattern on the wood and cut out the shape on the band saw (see pattern on page 27). The band saw table should form a perfect 90-degree angle to the blade.

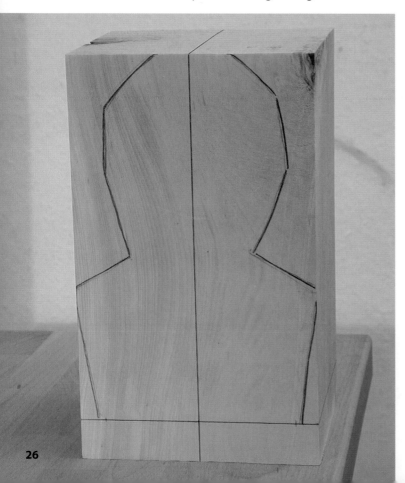

▲**3** Using a measuring device of your choice, draw a vertical line through the middle of the cutout as a guideline and mark the corresponding guideline on the model to re-establish the center of the project. **Note:** The guideline goes through the hollow of the throat.

Hollow of Throat

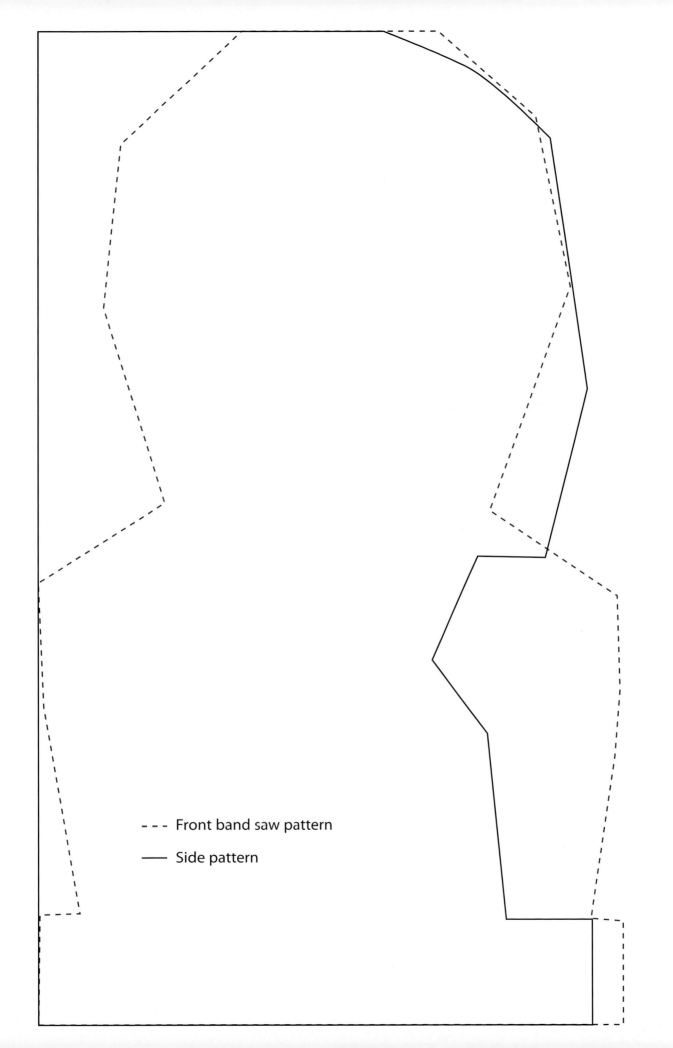

- - - Front band saw pattern

—— Side pattern

Part Three: The First Stage of Carving

◀ ▼ **4** Drill a hole on the bottom of the cutout for the carving screw and fix the cutout to the bench. If you are not familiar with this system, you may prefer to mount the cutout on a vise. Here we are using Stubai's 250 mm carving screw, since it is strong and suitable for most work.

Cutting the profile view

▼ **5** Draw the pattern of the profile (see page 27) and mark the line of the base on the wood.

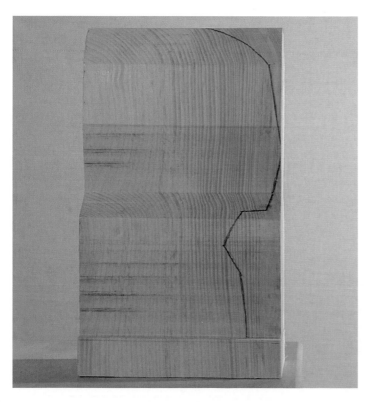

▲ **6** Using the #3-40 mm (shown here) and the #11-30 mm gouges, remove the excess material.

8 Compare the thickness on the edges of the block to check whether you have removed equal amounts of material from both sides of the profile.

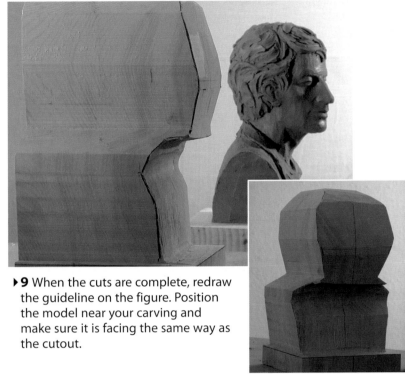

7 Try to make long cuts; it will help you to achieve consistency in the depth of your cuts. The base should remain untouched. The #11-30 mm gouge is being used in this photo. **Note:** Take care not to chip the base at the front!

9 When the cuts are complete, redraw the guideline on the figure. Position the model near your carving and make sure it is facing the same way as the cutout.

Fixing the profile

Fixing the angle of the profile is perhaps one of the most important steps in carving; it sets the foundation for the correct view. If this step is followed strictly, the chance of making mistakes in proportion or in the basic symmetry of the piece will be much less likely.

10 You have already marked the vertical guideline on both the model and the wood. Remember that the centerline of the face is approximately 30 degrees from the guideline. To mark the correct position of the nose, hold the calipers vertically and measure the height of the tip of the nose on the centerline of the model.

Using Calipers

To mark the correct position of the profile on the wood requires a special process that we will discuss here. First, we would like to make a few general points about using a measuring tool called calipers (also called dividers). At the Geisler-Moroder Austrian Woodcarving School, we often notice that many advanced carvers do not know how to use this tool correctly.

A set of calipers provides an ideal method for transferring measurements from your model to your carving. It should be used at any stage of carving when you need to make a mark or feel unsure about proportions or positioning. Calipers for a carver is like a walking stick for a mountain climber: It is always there to support. It is better to check your measurements once too often than once too few!

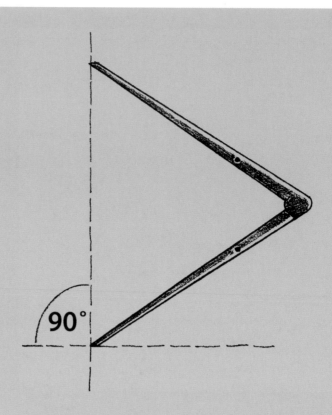

90°

Imagine the figure as if it were enclosed in a glass box. Measure from point to point, but measure along the walls of the imaginary glass box. For accurate measurement, it is important to always hold the calipers at a right angle to the plane. Holding the calipers against the nose and the base, for example, would give you an incorrect measurement.

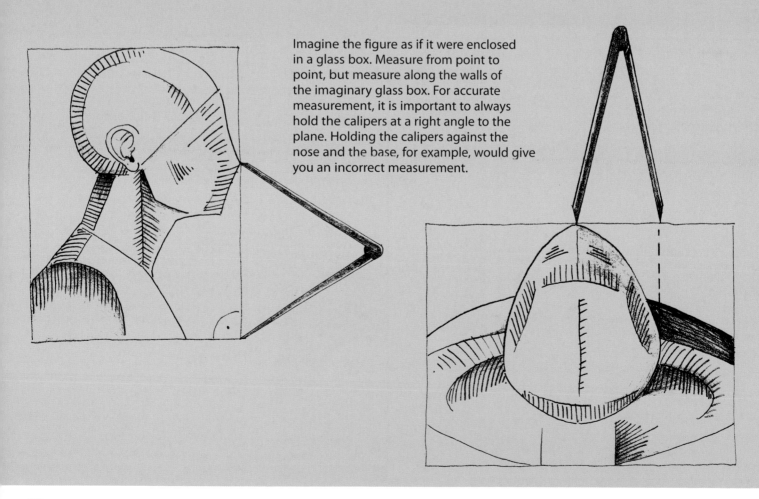

▶ **11** Transfer this measurement to the wood. **Note:** Hold the calipers at a perfect 90-degree angle!

▼ ▶ **12** On the model, measure from the tip of the nose to the guideline. Transfer this measurement to the wood. Remember to hold the calipers as if you were measuring through a glass plane; otherwise, the measured distance will not be accurate.

The Geisler-Moroder Austrian Woodcarving School Way

We do not cut the back of the figure until the very end. Leaving the material on gives the carver a certain amount of flexibility and freedom. If he is not entirely satisfied with the result of the face carving, he can always cut the face back and recarve it—as long as there is enough material left!

Part Three: The First Stage of Carving

Cutting the first planes

In our carving method at the Geisler-Moroder Austrian Woodcarving School, we work with planes. This means that we imagine every element as being surrounded by planes, and as we go along with the carving, ever-smaller planes will close around each element. Naturally, the first planes are always very big. Once you understand the concept of working with planes, you will be able to employ a very clear, systematic method of carving.

The basic cuts in this section turn the head to the correct angle and set the position of the nose, the forehead, and the mouth area. These first planes have to be very accurate because they set the correct angle of the head. Any mistake at this stage dramatically affects the final outcome of the carving.

▶**13** Start with the neck area by cutting the shoulders. Try to make long, wide, and clear sweeps with the gouge. Ideally, one plane is one cut; but of course, your ability to make this cut depends on not only your skill level, but also the size of the tool. Use as large a #3 gouge as you can!

▲ ▶**14** The next cuts set the planes for the side of the face. Make sure that these planes run from the side of the head to the nose, leaving only the necessary amount of wood for the width of the bridge of the nose. Make sure that the sides of these cuts are straight and symmetrical to the centerline and do not twist inward or outward.

▲**15** These cuts set the nose and the forehead. Establish the area from the tip of the nose to the top of the forehead with a flat cut.

▲**16** The next plane runs from the nose tip to the chin.

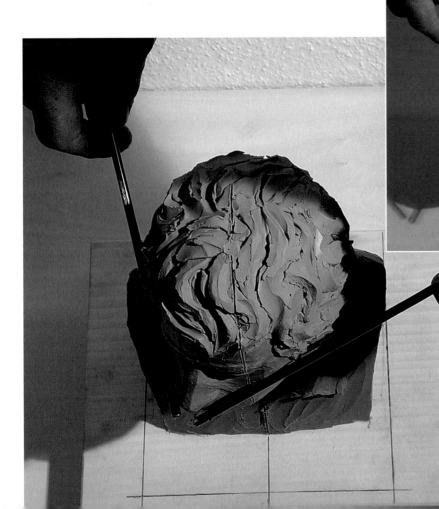

◄ ▲**17** Measuring the model will help you to define the depth of these cuts. Check the carving from the front, the sides, and above. Looking down at the carving, the angle of the profile should look like the angle shown in these photos.

▲18 The last big plane forms the front of the head at the hairline, starting from the hairline and moving up toward the top of the head.

▼19 Now, the piece is ready for the next step: marking proportional lines and dividing the face into three large areas in preparation for carving the features.

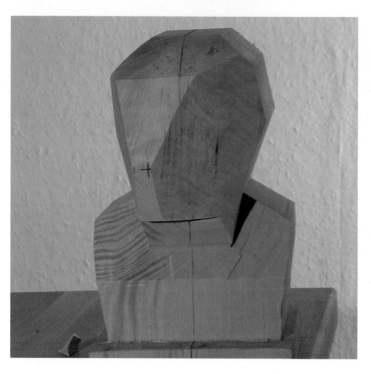

The planes of the neck

▶20 To position the basic shapes, transfer the centerline of the face from the model to the wood. As you did on the model before, now mark the basic proportional lines on the wood: mark one-fifth from the top of the head to define the hairline, and then divide the rest of the head into three parts. The third marking line should fall under the tip of the nose. Measure one-third the length of the head down from the chin to define the length of the neck.

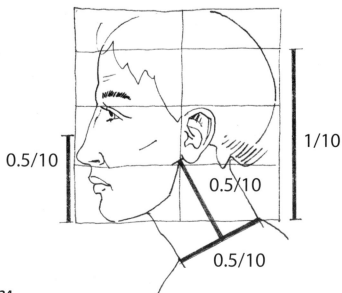

▲**21** With the #3-40 mm gouge, make a plane cut in at the neck from two sides. These cuts establish the planes for the sterno-mastoid muscles, which run from behind the ear to the hollow of the throat. Create two other planes to define the throat. Remove some wood between the Adam's apple and the hollow of the throat to achieve the required depth. Last, with two symmetrical cuts, shape the collar of the shirt. Your carving should look like the one pictured here.

▲**22** Do not cut the back of the carving at this point. The back will be cut once we have completed—and are satisfied with—the front of the carving.

▶**23** Double-check the profile of your carving against the one pictured here. Make any adjustments before moving on to the second stage of carving.

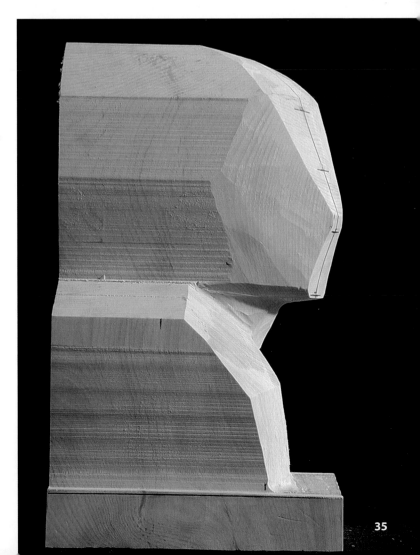

Part Four
The Second Stage of Carving

The following steps will take you from roughing out to defined geometric planes. In this section, we will further define the geometric planes that we roughed in during the first part. This stage will bring us closer to a realistic representation of the head.

Tools and Materials
- #3-40 mm gouge
- #11-10 mm gouge
- #11-20 mm gouge
- Other chisels and gouges of choice
- Calipers
- Mallet
- Carving screw
- Pencil

Part Four: The Second Stage of Carving

Setting the forms of the nose, the mouth, and the chin

We'll begin the second stage of carving by focusing on the placement of the nose, the mouth, and the chin—and making sure that they are symmetrical on the face. After this is completed, you will see the facial features starting to take shape.

▸**1** To set the forms along the proportional lines, first gouge out wood under the nose with the #11-10 mm gouge. Repeat the same cut above the nose. **Note:** Aim to set a symmetrical foundation for the features.

▾**2** To blend the top of the bridge of the nose into the gouge cut above it, use the #3-40 mm gouge.

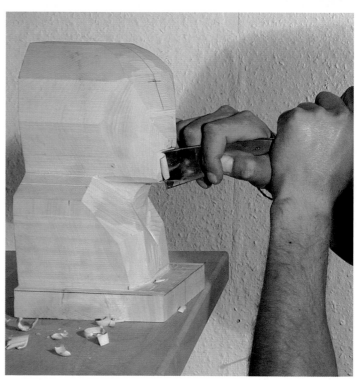

▴**3** With the same gouge, deepen the mouth and chin area.

38

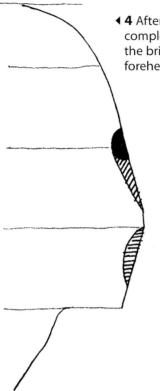

◀ **4** After these cuts have been completed, the angle between the bridge of the nose and the forehead becomes slightly wider.

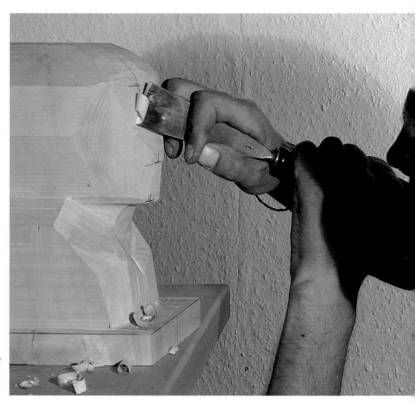

▶ **5** Next, free the top of the nose bridge by lowering the forehead.

▾ **6** Now continue working on the mouth and chin area. Divide the distance between the nose and the tip of the chin into three parts. The first line marks the place of the mouth; the second one is the hollow of the chin.

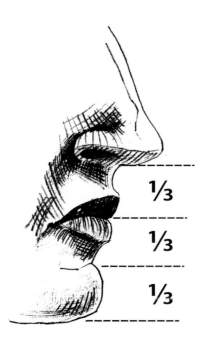

▴ **7** Using #11-10 mm gouge, gouge under the line of the mouth to raise the lower lip.

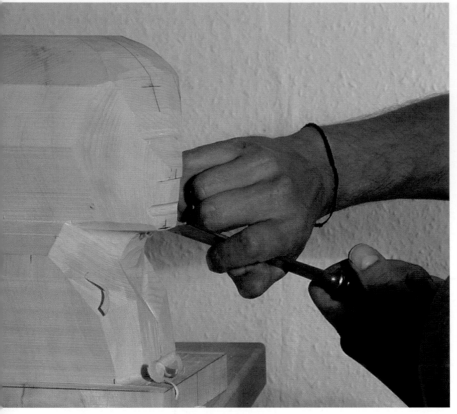

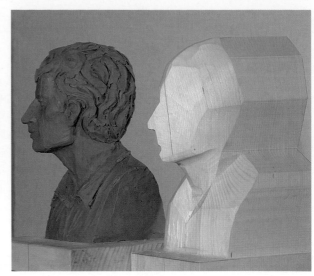

▲**9** Compare the model to the carving. The forms should be identical in placement. A face is starting to emerge.

▲**8** Round the chin with a large #3 gouge.

Setting the forms of the eyes and the hairline

Great care must be taken in the following steps to maintain symmetry, so a set of calipers is used often to measure the placement of the eyes and the hairline on the carving as compared to the model. The eyes are an important feature of any face, and carving them correctly will bring your creation to life.

▶**10** Make stop cuts on the lines marked under the eyes using a #3-40 mm gouge. These cuts will keep your gouge from splitting the wood of the eyes as you make the next cut. Now, under the eyes, cut along the sides of the nose with the gouge toward the eyes.

▼ ▶**11** Gouge along the stop cuts under the eyes with a #11-10 mm gouge, carving from the outside corners of the eyes to the inner corners.

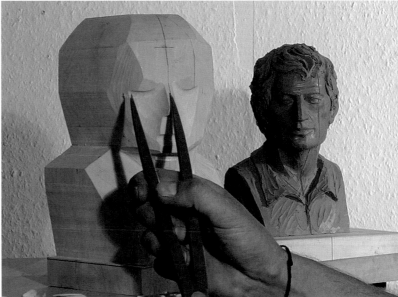

◀ ▲**12** Using calipers, check the width and the depth of the eyes' positions and compare these to the model. A typical mistake is for a beginning carver to carve the eyes too flat. As we mentioned before, the shape of the eyes resembles peach stones and the corners of the eyes should be really deep and almond shaped. Cutting the width of the bridge too small between the eyes is also a common mistake.

The Geisler-Moroder Austrian Woodcarving School Way

Because each carver's piece has tiny differences due to skill level and creativity, there is no preprinted pattern for the back of the head. We freehand it onto the carving, matching the proportions on the back to those on the front of the face.

▶ **13** Now, measure the hairline with the calipers and draw the hairline on the wood figure, preparing it for the next cuts.

▼ **14** Run a #11-10 mm gouge along the marked hairline.

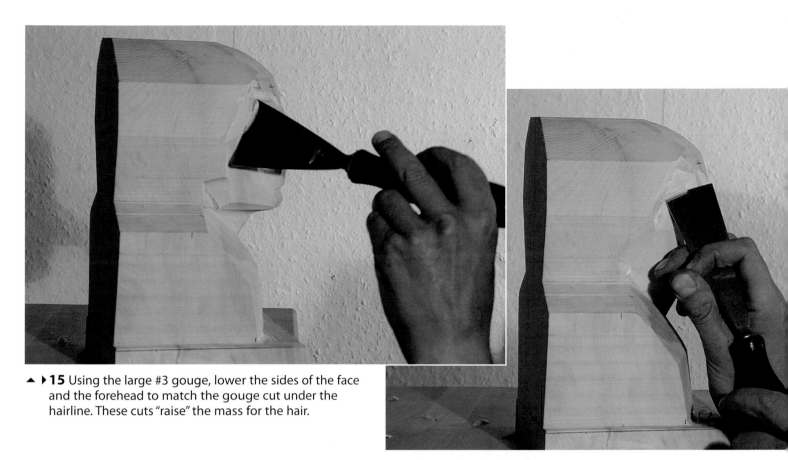

▲ ▸ **15** Using the large #3 gouge, lower the sides of the face and the forehead to match the gouge cut under the hairline. These cuts "raise" the mass for the hair.

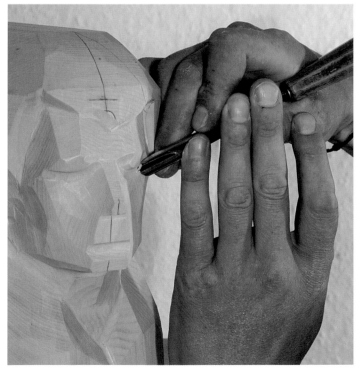

▲ **16** To complete the process of setting the forms, fix the corners of the eyes with a #11-10 mm gouge.

▲ **17** Check the model from all sides and correct any asymmetry in the features you may find. Now, the bust should look like the one pictured here. On the next pages, we will show you how to cut the sides and the back of the figure.

Part Four: The Second Stage of Carving

The sides of the head, the shoulders, and the collar

▲ **18** To complete the neck, transfer the line of the collar from the model to the carving with a pencil. Gouge under the line with the #11-10 mm gouge. Clean out the excess wood under the collar with the large #3 to match the gouge line and to raise the collar. Remember to check the measurements with the calipers to determine the position of the collar and the parameters of the head.

▲ **19** Now, reduce the material on the sides of the head with a few wide gouge cuts. Aim to achieve the round form of the head on the sides, just like those found on the corresponding areas of the model.

▲ **20** Before moving on to cut the back of the head, lower the shoulders. First, raise the head from the shoulders by gouging the sides of the neck and the shoulders with the #11-20 mm gouge. Round the shoulders slightly with the large #3 gouge.

▲ **21** To finish the work on the side view, round the top of the head with a few large gouge cuts. **Note:** Do not cut the back at this stage!

Carving the back

Once you are happy with the way the face has turned out, you are ready to cut the back. To create this section of the project, you will be working with proportions and matching the measurements of the back of the head to those on the front of the face. Be sure to use your own creativity as well; the carving should look aesthetically pleasing to you.

▲**22** Stop here and compare your carving to the photos above and to the model. Are you happy with the face? If not, now is the time to recarve it, before we cut the back.

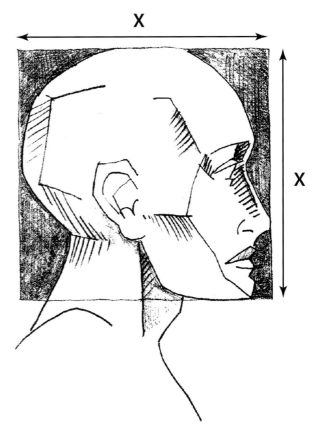

▲**23** To establish the depth of the head, it may help if you imagine a square around the head. The distance between the tip of the nose and the back of the head is the same as the distance between the level of the chin and the top of the head.

◄ **24** Draw the outline of the back on the figure, as shown in the picture.

25 Remove the excess wood on the back of the head and the neck with the large #3 gouge.

26 If necessary, make a few more cleaning cuts to complete the second stage of carving.

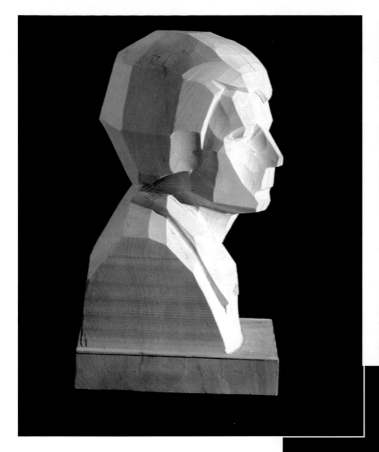

27 Now, the bust should look like this.

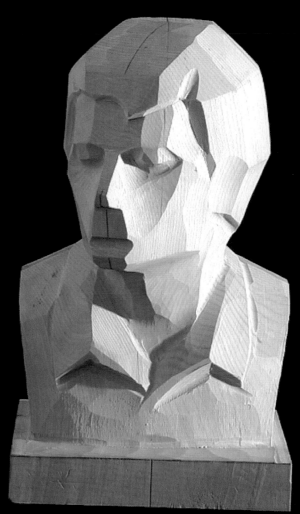

Part Five
The Third Stage of Carving

The following steps will take you from defined geometric shapes to finished piece. In this stage, we will "release" the final head from the geometric shapes. We'll also perform the final shaping cuts, giving the details of the carving their final forms.

Tools and Materials
- #3-20 mm gouge
- #3-40 mm gouge
- #5-20 mm gouge
- #7-10 mm gouge
- #7-20 mm gouge
- #9-20 mm gouge
- #11-10 mm gouge
- Other chisels and gouges of choice
- Calipers
- Mallet
- Carving screw
- Pencil

Part Five: The Third Stage of Carving

Detailing the nose, the mouth, and the chin

◀ **1** The first cuts will detail the nose. With a #7-10 mm gouge, shape the wing of the nose. **Note:** Maintaining the symmetry of the features is crucial for the harmonious appearance of the face.

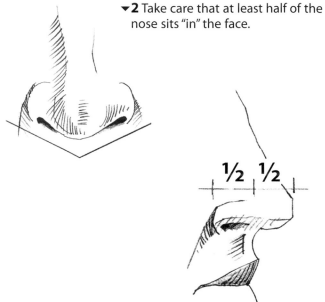

▼ **2** Take care that at least half of the nose sits "in" the face.

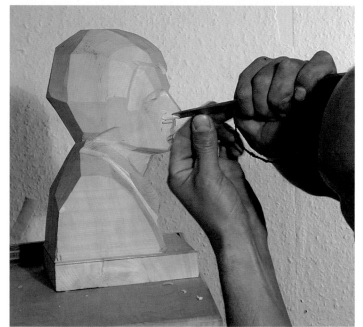

▲ **3** Using the same tool, cut gentle curves to indicate the nostrils underneath.

▶ **4** Cut both sides of the nose. We carved only one side of the nose first to show you the difference between the detailed nose and the nose before the cut. (A comparison photograph showing the carved and detailed wings is shown in Step 12 on page 53.)

▸**5** Now, we turn our attention to the mouth. To continue shaping this area, we will use a #3-20 mm gouge. Reduce the material on the side of the chin slightly to match the gouge cut from the previous step. Compare this illustration with the illustration in Part 2, Step 16 on page 16.

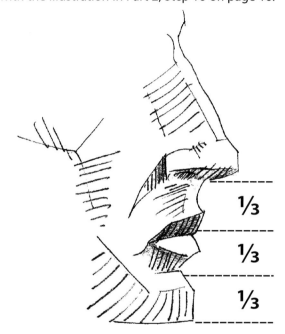

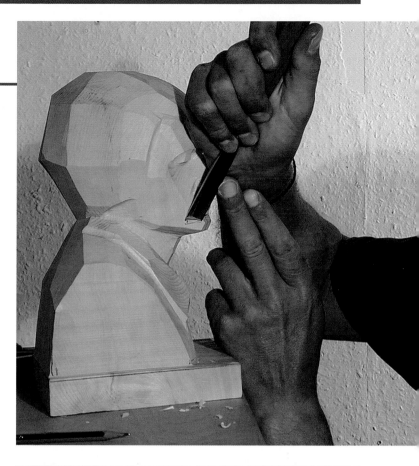

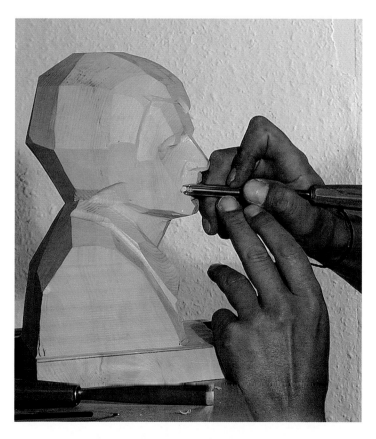

▲**7** This photo shows the mouth before and after the cuts.

◂**6** Note that the earlier gouge cut between the nose and the chin was positioned under the mouth. Now, check the width of the mouth with the calipers, and make a gouge cut right on the mouth line with the #11-10 mm gouge.

Part Five: The Third Stage of Carving

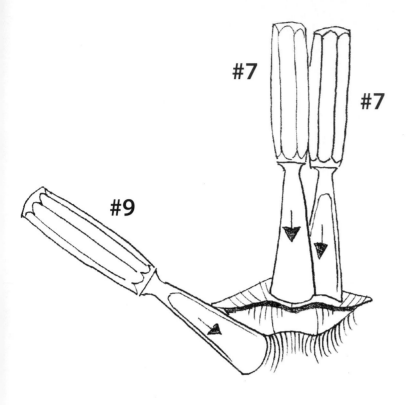

8 When carving the mouth, take care to emphasize the volume of the lips. After the sweep with the #11 gouge, shape the upper lip with a #7-20 mm gouge to create the line and the mounds of the lip. If necessary, scoop away a little more material under the lower lip to raise the volume with a #9-20 mm gouge.

9 With a #3-20 mm gouge, round the area under the lip.

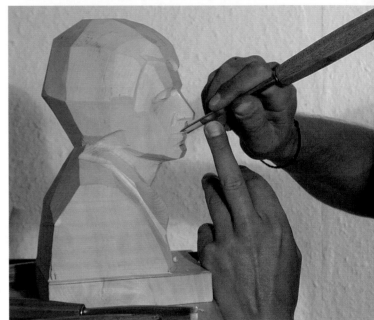

10 Here, you can see the mouth before and after the last cuts.

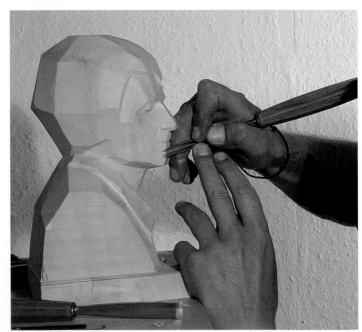

11 When the mouth is completed, shape the middle of the chin with a #11-10 mm gouge.

▲ 12 After the last shaping cuts, the bust with the detailed nose, mouth, and chin should look like the one shown here.

▸ 13 To position the ears correctly, mark two parallel horizontal lines: one at the bottom of the nose, the other at the top of the nose. The ears are positioned between these two lines, level with the nose. Compare this illustration to Part 2, Step 14 on page 14.

▾ 14 Draw the ears on the carving using the calipers. Use the illustration as a reference.

Shaping the ears

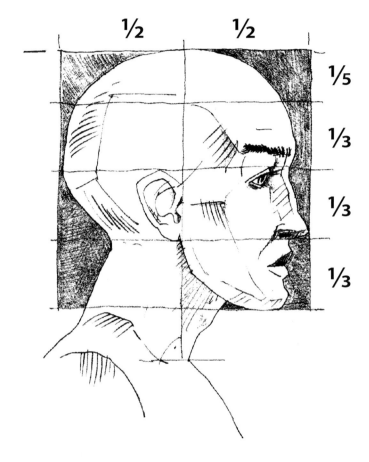

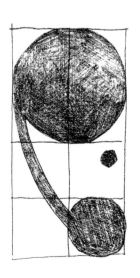
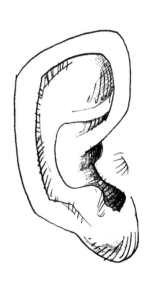

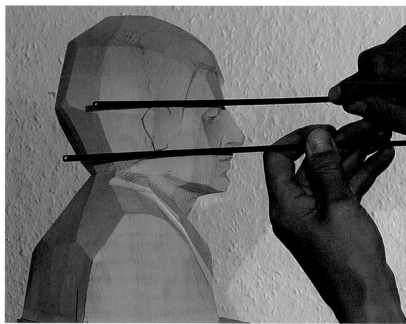

Part Five: The Third Stage of Carving

◀ **15** Carve around the ears with a #11-10 mm.

▼ **16** Continue shaping the outlines with a #5-20 mm gouge.

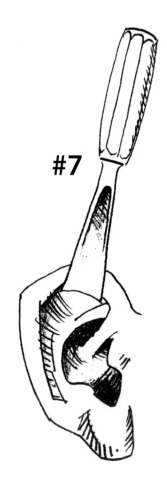

#7

◀ **17** Draw the inside of the ear and cut the curve of the ear with a #7 gouge.

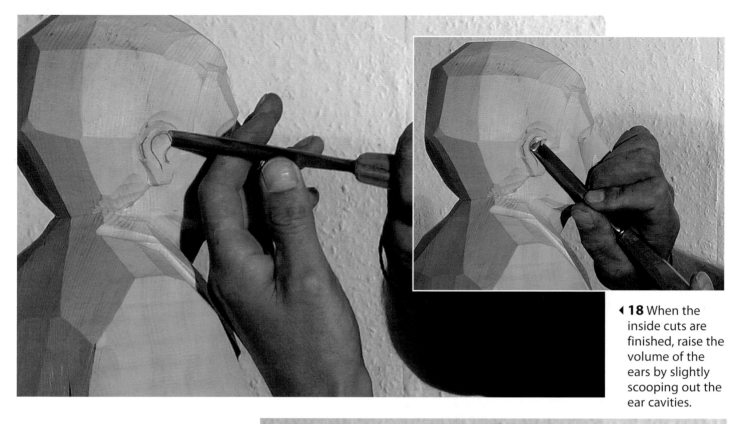

◀ **18** When the inside cuts are finished, raise the volume of the ears by slightly scooping out the ear cavities.

▶ **19** Upon completing the ears, the main part of the carving is finished. On the next pages, we will show you the finishing touches, such as texturing the hair and carving the base.

Part Five: The Third Stage of Carving

The finishing touches: the hair, the collar, and the base

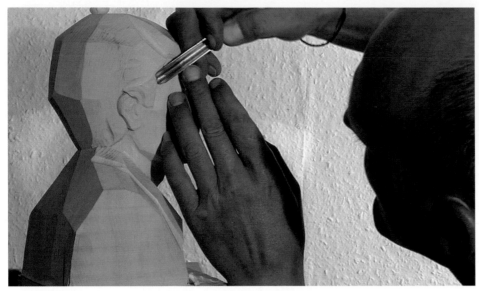

▲**20** Here, we show a very simple technique indicating only the main folds of the hair. Using the #11-10 mm, gouge out a few wavy lines with long, clean cuts.

21 Now, it is time for the rest of the small cuts, such as those that complete the collar at the back. Use the #11-10 mm gouge to cut under the outline and the #3-40 mm gouge to reduce the material under the collar. Where it is necessary, make a few cleaning cuts with a #3-40 mm gouge.

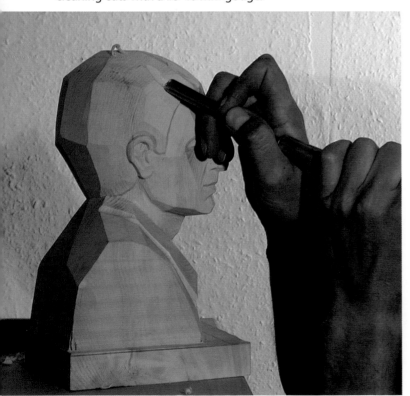

▲**22** To carve the base, use a large #3 gouge. At the front, you need to cut the base only as far back as the line of the chin. Do not reduce the material at the back or at the sides of the base; only make a few cleaning cuts.

◄ ▼**23** The finished carving. Now your work of art is ready for viewing in the round. You can stop here and declare your piece finished, or you can continue on to the next section for a variety of ideas on how to put a "final finish" on your carving.

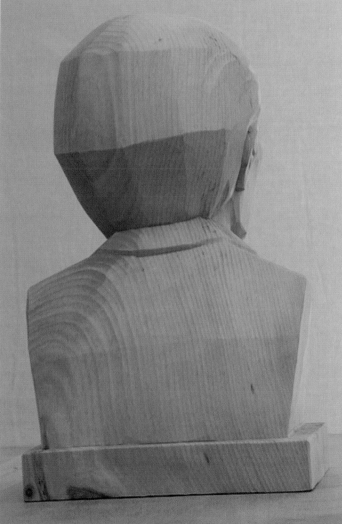

Part Six
The Final Finish – A Gallery of Ideas

This section will take you from the finished piece to the final details. Now we have the completed bust! If you have come this far, you have done the major part of the work, and, if you have followed our instructions, you are probably holding in your hands an excellent piece of carving already! We hope that you are satisfied with the result and that you have learned some new techniques during the process. We tried to give you a sense of the carving methods that we use at the Geisler-Moroder Austrian Woodcarving School, and we've passed on some "tricks" of this traditional, and yet so modern, system of the trade.

As you have probably noticed, the completed carving is not as detailed as our model. We've done this because we would like to show you a number of different possibilities for the final finish. In this chapter, you will see eight variations in further carving and three in surface treatment, such as staining, painting, and gilding. Realistic techniques are only a part of the possible finishes.

Usually, the finish of a woodcarving depends on the individual carver's style and on his choice of visual expression for communicating any planned messages. It is important for each carver to realize which techniques suit him best. Some carvers may like to experiment with new ideas and to enjoy unusual effects. Others may prefer realistic approaches. Whatever your goals are, you can find some useful ideas collected here in the gallery.

The teachers of our school completed the busts in the gallery. They developed their own interpretations of the carving that you completed by working through the pages of this book. These carvings represent some of the most popular areas of surface treatment. Most of the carved busts were left natural and only oiled or waxed (we used Danish oil and colorless buffer wax). However, three of them received further treatments, such as painting and gilding.

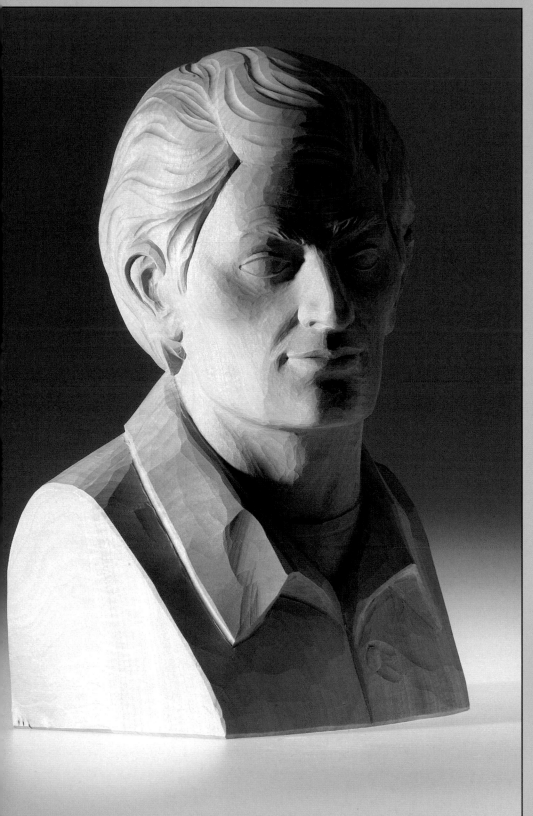

Horst Pali

Horst Pali gave a realistic finish to this bust of a young man. Please notice the added details on the eyes, nose, mouth, and ears. He carved this piece to match the original model in this book as closely as possible.

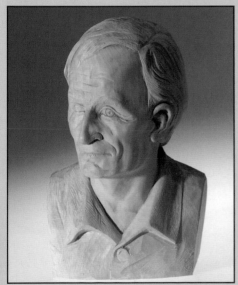

Michael Bachnetzer

Michael Bachnetzer's bust is a realistic style interpretation. He portrayed a man in his fifties. The skin on the face looks less firm. There are wrinkles around the eyes and deep furrows on the brow, around the nose, and at the corners of the mouth. The hairline has retreated. The expression of the sculpture challenges the process of aging.

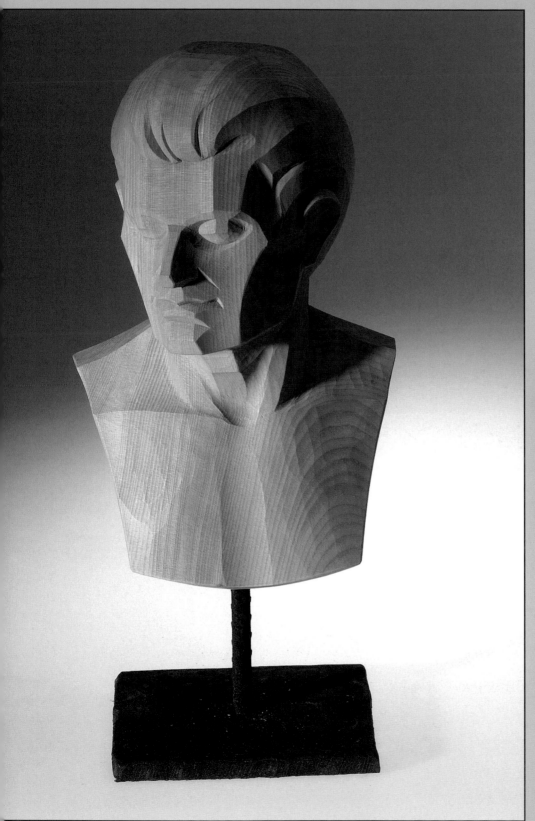

Horst Pali

This bust by Horst Pali received a stylized finish. He carved the features as if they were surrounded by planes and used only a minimal amount of cuts to describe the character. The cuts follow the anatomical structure of the face, giving a strong emphasis to the muscles and the bones. The result is an abstract appearance. He mounted the bust on an iron base to create a light and decorative arrangement.

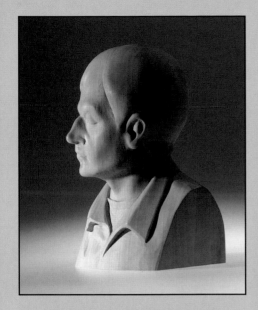

Michael Bachnetzer

Michael Bachnetzer gave a very smooth and soft finish to this bust. He used sandpaper through 250 grit. Using this finish, he portrayed an ageless and distant man. The figure seems to be in another realm, or at least surrounded by mist. Mysterious appearances are often carved with this "soft and smooth" technique.

Pascal Wirth

Pascal Wirth's figure feels very much as if it is flesh and blood. He portrayed a man dressed in the fashion characteristic of the 1960s. To create this character, he applied many different textures. This extensive use of texturing lends an energetic and lively appearance to sculptures.

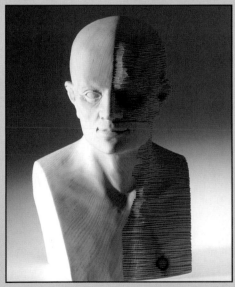

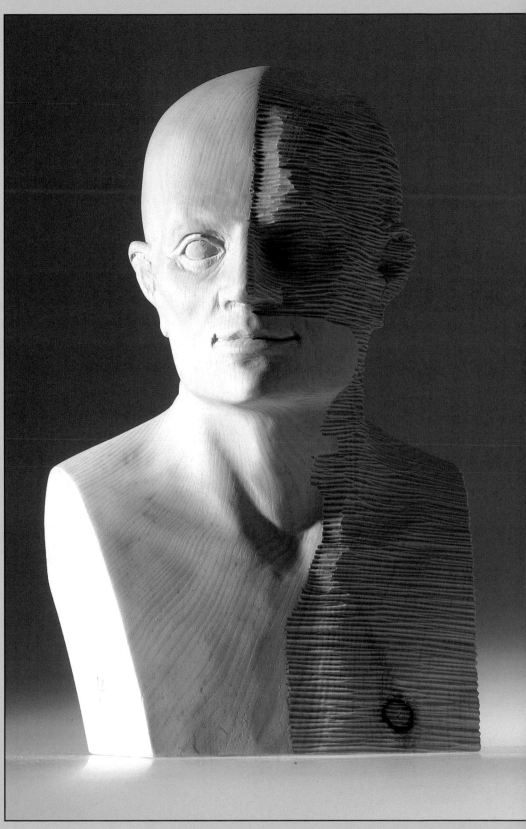

Gottfried Kaschnig

Gottfried Kaschnig carved this bust as if the character wore a half-mask. He created the effect by using a V-tool to texture short parallel grooves in the area of the mask. As a contrast, he used fine-grit sandpaper to smooth the other half of the face. Interesting solution!

Robert Simon

Robert Simon often combines wood with different materials, such as glass or metal, in his sculptures. His interpretation of the bust invites spectators into the secret and complicated inner spaces of the human head. This variation shows a way of extending woodcarving into other areas of sculpturing.

Horst Pali – Woodcarving
Bernhard Tragut – Painting

Bernhard Tragut painted Horst Pali's carved bust with an "antique painting" technique. The paint is applied on several layers of gesso that is established over many hours. This technique is traditionally used in churches to color sculptures, and mastering it takes lots of patience, time, and special skills on the part of the artist.

Pascal Wirth – Woodcarving
Claudia Grutsch – Painting

Here is Pascal Wirth's figure painted in the "Geisler-Moroder way." At the Geisler-Moroder Austrian Woodcarving School, we often paint the wood only with watercolors mixed with stain—a technique that leaves the colors so transparent that the grains of the wood can show through. Discover the natural beauty of this technique for yourself!

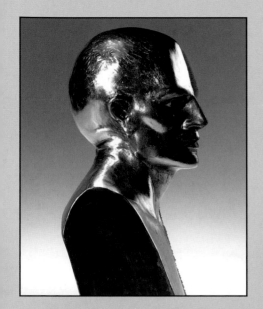

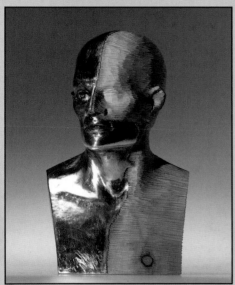

Gottfried Kaschnig –Woodcarving
Bernhard Tragut - Painting

Here is an alternate finish on Gottfried Kaschnig's carving. The bust is gilded with the traditional technique we use at the Geisler-Moroder Austrian Woodcarving School. After applying many layers of gesso, Bernhard Tragut covered the surface with real silver leaves. Around the area of the mouth and the eyes, he oxidized the silver to emphasize the character. The effect is stunning!

Markus Treml

Markus Treml finished two of the busts in an extremely stylized way. He is a well-known artist in Austria, and he strives to understand human nature. He is more interested in the function of the human head than in its outward appearance. He tried to express this quest in the two stylized busts.

The first one depicts the human head as a book of knowledge and memories, emphasizing the eye as an important organ for accessing information. "Watch and learn!" Markus says with his sculpture.

The second piece of Markus' is a variation on the first idea. What happens if the pages of the "human book" are not flat but instead are three-dimensional? The result is fascinating—a completely different sculpture!

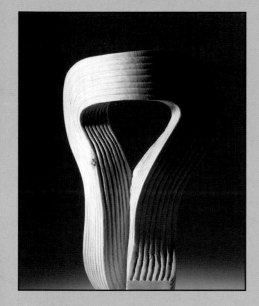

Appendix A

Metric Conversion Chart

Millimeter	Inch		Millimeter	Inch
1 mm	$\frac{1}{32}$"		40 mm	1 $\frac{9}{16}$"
2 mm	$\frac{1}{16}$"		50 mm	2"
3 mm	$\frac{3}{32}$"		55 mm	2 $\frac{3}{16}$"
4 mm	$\frac{1}{8}$"		60 mm	2 $\frac{3}{8}$"
5 mm	$\frac{3}{16}$"		70 mm	2 $\frac{3}{4}$"
6 mm	$\frac{1}{4}$"		80 mm	3 $\frac{1}{8}$"
7 mm	$\frac{1}{4}$"		85 mm	3 $\frac{3}{8}$"
8 mm	$\frac{5}{16}$"		90 mm	3 $\frac{9}{16}$"
9 mm	$\frac{3}{8}$"		100 mm	3 $\frac{15}{16}$"
10 mm	$\frac{3}{8}$"		110 mm	4 $\frac{5}{16}$"
11 mm	$\frac{7}{16}$"		120 mm	4 $\frac{11}{16}$"
12 mm	$\frac{1}{2}$"		130 mm	5 $\frac{1}{8}$"
13 mm	$\frac{1}{2}$"		140 mm	5 $\frac{1}{2}$"
14 mm	$\frac{9}{16}$"		150 mm	5 $\frac{7}{8}$"
15 mm	$\frac{9}{16}$"		160 mm	6 $\frac{5}{16}$"
16 mm	$\frac{5}{8}$"		170 mm	6 $\frac{11}{16}$"
17 mm	$\frac{11}{16}$"		180 mm	7 $\frac{1}{16}$"
18 mm	$\frac{3}{4}$"		190 mm	7 $\frac{1}{2}$"
19 mm	$\frac{3}{4}$"		195 mm	7 $\frac{11}{16}$"
20 mm	$\frac{13}{16}$"		200 mm	7 $\frac{7}{8}$"
21 mm	$\frac{13}{16}$"		210 mm	2 $\frac{1}{4}$"
22 mm	$\frac{7}{8}$"		220 mm	8 $\frac{11}{16}$"
23 mm	$\frac{7}{8}$"		230 mm	9 $\frac{1}{16}$"
24 mm	$\frac{15}{16}$"		240 mm	9 $\frac{7}{16}$"
25 mm	1"		250 mm	9 $\frac{13}{16}$"
30 mm	1 $\frac{3}{16}$"		260 mm	10 $\frac{1}{4}$"

Appendix B — Illustrations

The following section includes the front, side, and back views of the model as well as proportional drawings that have been enlarged for your reference. Use these to aid you as you carve the project in this book as well as any future projects.

Model – Front

Model – Side

Model – Back

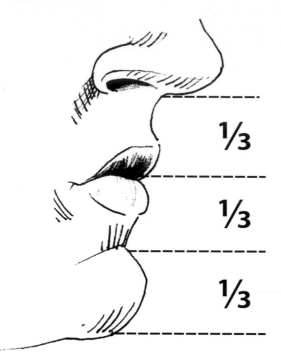

Proportions of the Lower Face

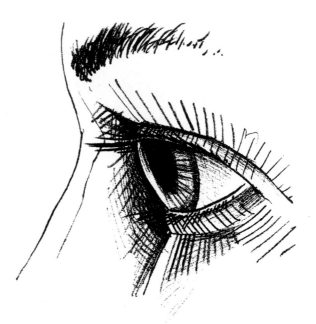

Curvature of the Eye

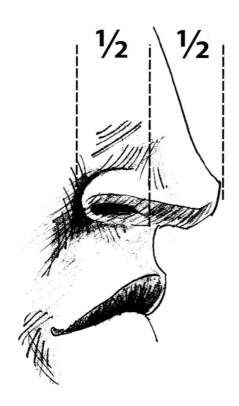

Proportions of the Nose

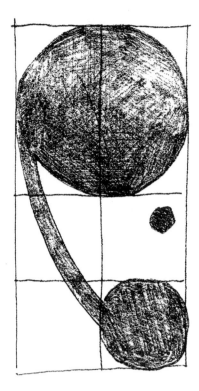

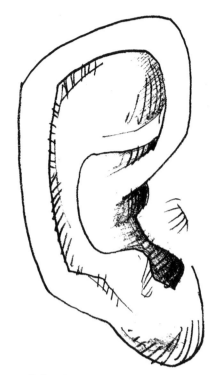

Shape of the Ear

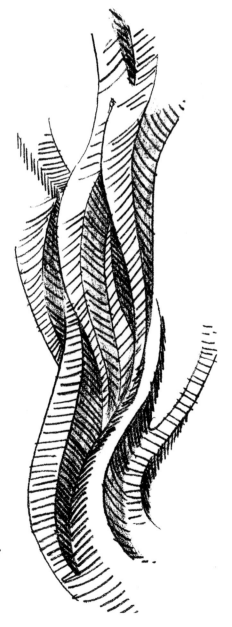

Texture of the Hair

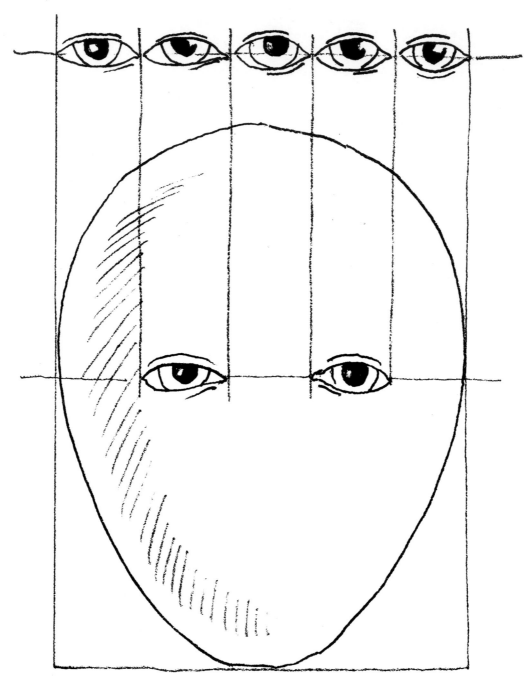

Placement of the Eyes

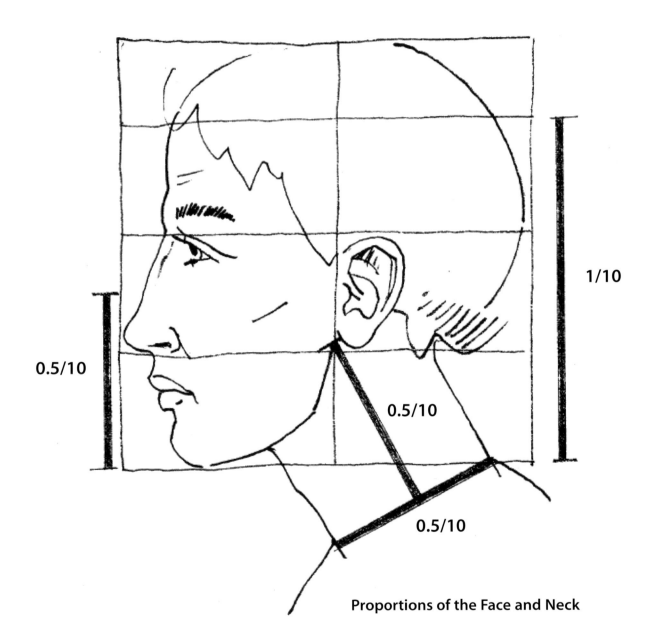

1/10

0.5/10

0.5/10

0.5/10

Proportions of the Face and Neck

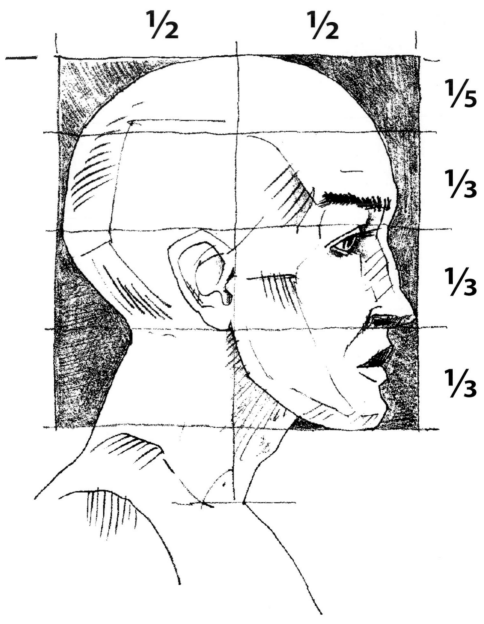

½ ½

⅕

⅓

⅓

⅓

Proportions of the Head

Proportions of the Head

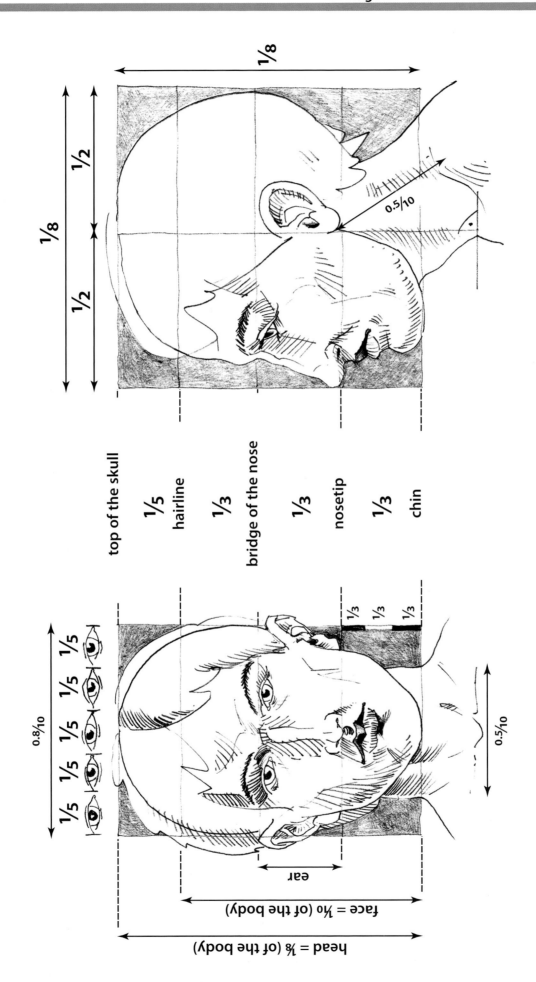

top of the skull

1/5 hairline

1/3 bridge of the nose

1/3 nosetip

1/3 chin

1/8

1/2

1/2

1/8

1/2

1/2

0.5/10

1/3
1/3
1/3

0.8/10

1/5 1/5 1/5 1/5 1/5 1/5 1/5

ear

0.5/10

face = 1/10 (of the body)

head = 1/8 (of the body)

1/8 = of the body (the head length is an eighth of the body)

1/10 = of the body (the face length is a tenth of the body)

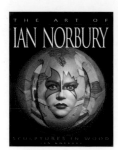

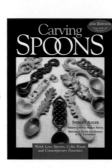
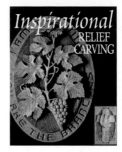